Experiments With Vacuum Tubes

Salomons

BIBLIOLIFE

EXPERIMENTS WITH VACUUM TUBES

BY

SIR DAVID L. SALOMONS, Bart., M.A.

PAST VICE-PRESIDENT OF THE INSTITUTION OF ELECTRICAL ENGINEERS,
FELLOW OF THE ROYAL ASTRONOMICAL SOCIETY,
ETC , ETC , ETC.

WITH 54 ILLUSTRATIONS

LONDON

WHITTAKER AND CO.

2, WHITE HART STREET, PATERNOSTER SQUARE, E C.

NEW YORK : 66, FIFTH AVENUE

1903

PREFACE

BEFORE leaving Cambridge, I had the good fortune to meet the late Mr. Spottiswoode, who charmed me by his beautiful experiments with vacuum tubes. Prior to that time I took a great interest in the subject, partly from the beauty of the phenomena, and partly because they seemed to baffle all efforts to unravel them.

From that day to this the subject has engrossed my attention, for I believed that a great deal could be done with these tubes, if only the right methods were devised.

At the time when Messrs. Gassiot, Warren De La Rue, Spottiswoode, Moulton and others were at work, their attempts to get at the bottom of the phenomena were conducted by means of high E M.F. and large currents. In fact, the very methods which they pursued confused the results, though interesting and instructive, and the procedure they adopted can only be compared to the fable of the " Frog and the Bull."

Coil after coil was made, each one larger than the preceding one, until the final one gave out (that at the Polytechnic), and no useful results were obtained.

1 ᕐ 1 1 ᕐ

For a time this class of work was dropped, probably because the idea obtained that nothing further could be done, or that nothing serviceable could result. Then Sir William Crookes entered the field with his new experiments, termed by him "radiant matter" phenomena, which so charmed the scientific world when the experiments were first shown.

More recently, Professor J. J. Thompson in his brilliant researches at Cambridge has been employing vacuum tubes.

For spectrum analysis the vacuum tube has always been of service.

The numerous experiments undertaken in the past were made chiefly to ascertain the cause for the formation of bands, and for the examination of the phenomena of electric discharge in rarefied gases.

Latterly modified Crookes tubes have been largely employed for X-ray work.

This little volume deals with a subject which appeals to a very small portion of the Public, and even to a limited number of those engaged in Science.

However, the results of the experiments about to be described, may prove of some interest to those who are working in the particular line with which this book treats.

I, therefore, for the benefit of the few, deem it right to publish the series of experiments which represent the labour of many years.

A very large number of experiments made with ordinary and with Crookes' vacuum tubes are not published here since the series is not yet complete, but I trust that, in due course, a supplementary volume will appear describing them.

It will be noticed in the following descriptions, that a totally different method has been followed to that used by those who have worked in the past, and the advantages to be derived therefrom are evident from the results.

I have made no attempt to propound a theory, though tempted to suggest possibilities in some instances. Such suggestions must not be taken to imply that I necessarily think no other reason or explanation as good or even better might be advanced, and they are offered to connect the chain of the subject in some intelligible manner.

EXPERIMENTS WITH VACUUM TUBES

PART I

THE vacuum tube, so called, is, as we all know, not a
vacuum tube, but a glass tube containing rarefied gas or
mixed gases. Therefore when speaking of vacuum tubes I
do so in its common sense and not as a definition of the
apparatus.

The chief advantage gained from the uses of vacuum
tubes, is in the fact that it is possible to see what is going
on without requiring supplementary apparatus.

To make comparisons between currents passing through
such tubes and through other conductors, it must first be
shown that the manner in which the current travels through
rarefied gases is similar in some, if not in all, respects to
the manner in which it travels through other conductors.

It is now believed that the current travels through a gas
after the same fashion as it does through a liquid. It is
further supposed that the manner in which a current
travels through a solid conductor, is different to the way in
which it traverses a liquid.

It is quite possible that the current flows through a
solid in the same way as it does through a liquid, though,
of course, other phenomena may at the same time be
produced due to the substance being a solid, which mask
the result.

In the year 1883 I conducted some exhaustive experiments with a view to ascertain whether a metal conductor was affected in any way by the passage of the current. Large and small wires were employed with various currents. The metals selected were copper, iron, German silver, platinum and silver. In all cases the metals were rendered crystalline and brittle. Authorities differ in their views as to whether the passage of the electric current renders a metal crystalline or not. I regard my experiments as conclusive that such is the case, but of course it is quite possible that the change may be produced by incidents due to the traverse of the current, and not to the current itself.

It seems difficult to conceive a reason why the current should pass from one point to another, through a gas, liquid, or solid, in completely different ways. It would appear more probable that the propagation in all cases is alike, and the differences in the phenomena are more hidden than real.

Whether such method of advance in all cases is the same or not, it is impossible to deny that numerous phenomena are common to the three classes named, and the phenomena which are common, are those which may be regarded as the most important.

We all know that, generally, bands of light are formed in a vacuum tube, which are stationary, if the E.M.F. of the current is absolutely steady, and these are present whether the current be a direct, an intermittent-direct, or an alternate one. We do not, however, know for certain whether the analogous phenomenon is produced in solid conductors. Professor Fleming has found that, if powdered coke and magnesia or chalk are mixed, they will, on passing an alternative current through them, become separated into layers, somewhat analogous to the bands produced in vacuum tubes; but the cause may be different In some of the Tesla experiments nodes are produced in the conductors, which may have some kind of relationship to the bands.

These results may or may not be a fair analogy, but of one thing we may be confident. It is, that the bright bands are due to heated matter and are not visible electricity. The very fact that these bands can be seen from all points of view, is sufficiently conclusive that such is the case.

That it is the passage of the current which causes these bands to appear, is also certain. If a single discharge is passed through a tube, the tube appears lit throughout for the moment and there the phenomenon ends. This is due to the persistence of vision. If the tube is examined with a rotating mirror, it is found that a band of light advances from end to end, at a speed approaching the rate at which light travels; yet when discharges are passed in rapid succession through the tube, the bands become more or less stationary, without any signs of advance.

A vast number of experiments have been made, to ascertain the nature of these bands. It would appear to me, that self-induction is probably the reason for their appearance; and, if I may so express myself, it is the various checks given to the advance of the successive discharges, which cause the matter in the tube to become heated to a high temperature; and the current in the darker portions travels freely without heating the matter present, or only to a slight degree. The current from an induction coil secondary is oscillatory as well as intermittent, which fact should not be lost sight of. Resonance would also be an explanation for the appearance of bands.

Rightly or wrongly, it appears to me that the current passing through the vacuum tube, when bands are produced, is analogous to a lightning discharge through a very good conductor, in which case self-induction retards the passage of the current.

Professor Hughes some years ago, was the first to point out a number of new phenomena in connection with unsteady currents, and to suggest that there would probably be an advantage in using iron, instead of copper, for lightning rods; and the vacuum tube experiments appear to me one of the means for confirming this view.

By varying the exhaustion in a vacuum tube, and consequently its resistance, many of these effects can be shown. I am thus led to the conclusion that it is quite possible, we see in the vacuum tube at least some of the phenomena which really do occur in other conductors. To put this more plainly in the instance given, if a tube is very little exhausted, the discharge has no band. When the resistance of the tube is greatly diminished, by further exhaustion, the bands appear, provided a suitable tube be chosen. Although I do not assume that the method of current propagation in rarefied gases and metal conductors is identical, I do think that there is much in common, especially if the modern view be accepted that the current travels by means of the dielectric and sinks into the conductor.

To investigate this subject, with practically no given data, the simplest course to pursue, was to obtain a large number of tubes, and sort them according to some phenomenon which appeared common to each set. It then occurred to me that by the adoption of the method, which has proved so successful in mathematics, viz. that of diminishing the quantity under examination to near the limit of its existence, might give better results than the methods employed by other investigators who tried rather to make the values infinite, were it possible.

By employing very small E.M.F. and very small

current, the difficulties which beset earlier investigators disappeared, and the phenomena were seen in their purity. Then on raising the E.M.F. successive super-added phenomena appeared, which would have been exceedingly puzzling, had the start not been made in the manner mentioned.

Briefly the following facts came to light :—

1. That the band produced, when the current passes over any small solid body, such as a disc glass, is double and not single.

A = Bright Bands.   B = Dark Spaces.

Bright bands A expanded overlap at dark spaces B, which now appear twice as bright as at A, and the spaces A appear dark by contrast.

Fig. 1.

2. That this double band may be considerably separated by elongating the disc, say, to let the disc become a short or a long rod. A long electrode also produces the effect.

3. That when the E.M.F. is not exceedingly small, the bright bands in the tube are spurious and are really situated at the dark spaces, which is due to the fact that the bright bands have expanded and overlapped, and that the dark spaces, which are the expanded bright bands, are only dark by contrast with the overlaps. (See Fig. 1.)

4. That this overlapping may be repeated again and

again as the E.M.F. is raised, the limit being the destruction of the tube.

5. That, if there is inserted at one end of the tube a rod, disc, contraction or diaphragm, or any other equivalent arrangement, bright bands are formed throughout the tube, at a distance apart; which is governed by the nature of the arrangement placed in the end of the tube.

6. That the glass of the tube appears to act, in some way, in forming the bands.

7. In a free tube the number of alternations may vary the number of the bands.

The knowledge of these various effects is a great assistance in pursuing this subject. It becomes possible to make

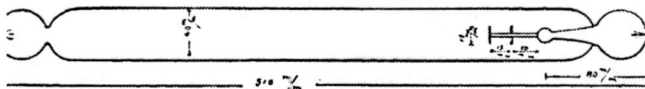

Fig. 2.

two or more tubes to give precisely the same phenomena. It is possible to make tubes giving narrow or wide bands at pleasure, and many of the experiments which will be spoken of later could not be performed with certainty unless such tubes could be made. Formerly it might have become necessary to manufacture 100 tubes before finding one that would answer the purpose ; and then to produce a second one, the same process would have to be gone through.

I do not wish to say more on the method of making the tubes beyond giving a few examples, as I have already published Papers on the subject, which are to be found in the *Proceedings of the Royal Society*, vol. 56, and elsewhere, and there all details are given.

Figs. 2, 3, and 4 represent vacuum tubes, of various

types, in each of which a little glass apparatus is inserted at one end. The bands will be produced throughout the

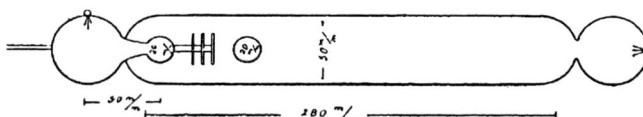

FIG 3.

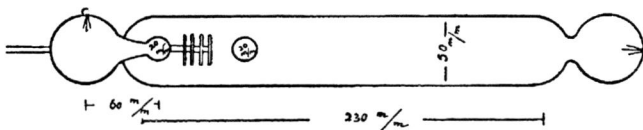

FIG. 4.

length of the free tube, at a distance apart equal to the distance between the glass discs.

Fig. 5 represents a special form of glass tube, wherein

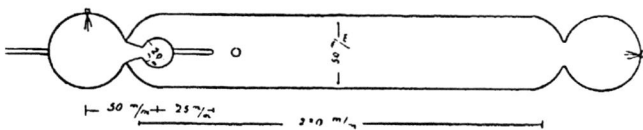

FIG. 5.

the bands will be produced at a distance apart, approximately equal to the length of the little rod seen at the end of the tube.

Fig. 6 shows a tube with a contraction. The bands will appear apart, at a distance equal to the length of the contraction.

Fig. 7 illustrates the tube with a diaphragm for producing bands at given distances, which in this case will be

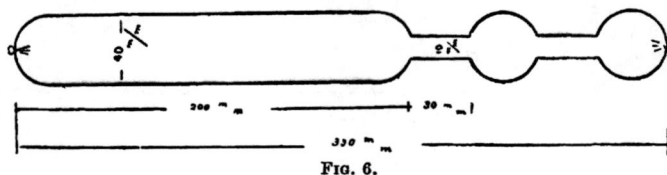

FIG. 6.

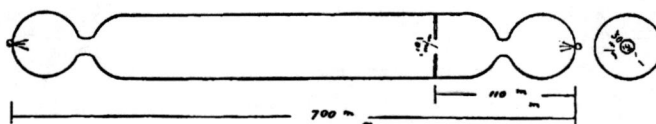

FIG. 7.

approximately equal to the distance beween the diaphragm and the electrode nearest to it.

Fig. 8 shows a tube lit by induction, there being no connection between the electrodes and the free portion of

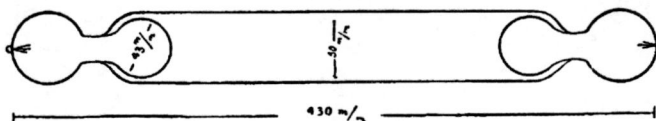

FIG. 8.

the tube, and the bands are formed at a distance apart which is regulated by the size of the inductive glass spheres.

Fig. 9 is a tube in which a little glass disc can be made to stand up, or lie down, at pleasure. The method of regulating the bands is perfectly shown in such a tube, using it first as an open tube, and then as one having a special arrangement for making the bands appear at a given distance apart. In this case the distance will be equal to the distance between the glass disc and its nearest electrode.

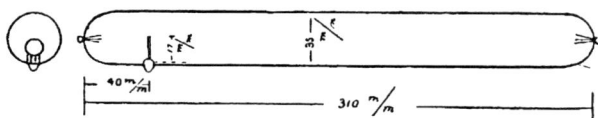

Fig. 9.

Professor Fleming, after seeing the tubes with fixed discs, etc., suggested that a tube might be constructed to show the action of what I term the "deflector" in one tube, and in consequence the form Fig. 9 was made.

If in a tube in which bands are formed, bulbs are blown along its length, the bands refuse to appear in the bulbs, which may be taken as an indication that the glass plays

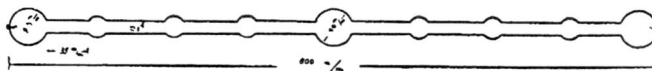

Fig. 10.

some part in their formation. If the tube consists of a large glass bulb in the course of a tube, it will be observed that little bands appear at an entrance to the bulb. They stick to the entrance, and are bulged into the bulb, and it requires some coaxing (increase of E.M.F.) to induce these bands to form in the bulb.

Fig. 10 is a tube with bulbs blown along its course. The bands will not form in the bulbs.

Fig. 11 exhibits a tube lit inductively, having a large sphere in the centre of its course.

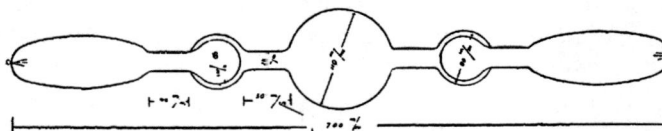

Fɪɢ. 11.

Fig. 12 shows the position of the bands with a small current passed in tube Fig 11.

Fig. 13 gives the appearance of the bands when the current is greatly increased in same tube. This experi-

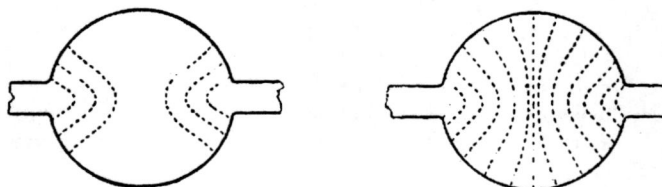

First Stage.

Fɪɢ. 12.

Second Stage.
(More current passed.)

Fɪɢ 13.

ment well illustrates the tendency of the bands to stick to the glass, and bears out my contention that the dielectric has a considerable influence in their formation.

Then with the "electric egg," which is so well known, on being exhausted to a considerable degree, the current passes in the centre as a column of light, and if matter is inserted in any quantity, which is usually done by introducing the vapour of alcohol, of naphtha, or of any other volatile fluid, bands will appear.

This would indicate that the matter present enables the current to reach the glass. Although frequently the bands may seem not to reach the glass, it can generally be shown that this is the case when they are present, but the fact of the eye not always seeing the effect does not necessarily prove that it is non-existent.

It might be imagined, from what I have said, that it is not uncommon for bands to be produced in a globe or tube

Fig. 14.

without reaching the sides of the glass, but it will be found no easy matter to produce the effect.

It must be remembered that in the electric egg the glass sides are very far removed from the electrodes, whereas in the case of the tube mentioned this is not so. But if, however, in a tube, say 300 mm. and 40 mm. diameter,

Fig. 15.

a little metal plate is placed across the tube, at about the centre of its length, this acts as a bridge, and the current discharge will now be very similar to, yet not identical with, that which takes place in the electric egg.

The following experiments illustrate the foregoing points. Fig. 14 contains rarefied air, and on passing a current a faint, unstriated light makes its appearance. Fig. 15 is a similar tube, but some alcohol vapour is

B

introduced. In this case closely-packed bands are produced. Fig. 16 is again, a similar tube with a platinum plate across the tube. When the current is passed, the discharge is almost similar to that in the electric egg.

The experiment of producing a radial discharge in vacuo, to give an appearance somewhat similar to that of "Newton's Rings," is a difficult one to produce, on account of the great care necessary in the construction of the

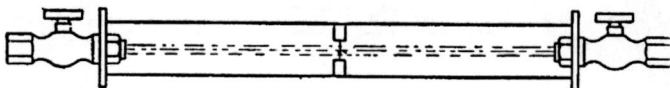

FIG 16.

apparatus. After many failures I succeeded in producing a tube which gives the desired result.

Two hemispheres of glass, the edges being carefully ground, are placed together with suitable grease, and they are so arranged that what becomes a glass sphere can be placed on an air pump to be exhausted.

Within this sphere and from below there is supported by a metal rod, surrounded by ebonite, a flat gun-metal saucer, in the bottom of which is placed a sheet of glass. The exposed inside of the saucer rim is employed as an electrode.

There is another rod in the upper portion of the sphere, also protected by ebonite, the lower end of the rod passing through a hole in a circular piece of glass and has a small cylindrical nut screwed on it to keep the glass on the rod, and this circular piece of glass fits exactly in the gun-metal saucer, and thus the small nut on the end of the rod is truly central with the inside rim of the saucer.

Consequently there is a central electrode, viz. the nut at the end of the rod, and a circular electrode being the inside of the rim of the saucer so much as is exposed between the two glass plates.

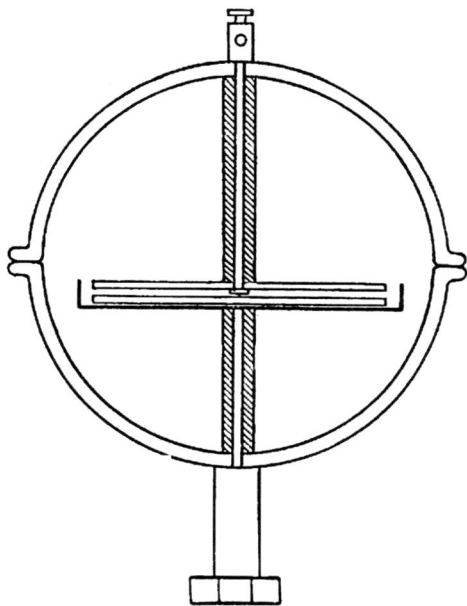

Fig. 17.

This space between the glass plates is equivalent to a vacuum tube, and suitable connections exist outside the glass sphere in order to make the connections with the secondary of the induction coil. Fig. 17 shows the arrangement.

A very small E.M.F. has to be employed in this experiment, the spark in air not exceeding 0·15 mm.

If the room is quite dark the whole of what appears to be the inside of the saucer becomes illuminated. To better see the effect, the inside of the saucer is blackened. Every now and then, if the phenomenon is carefully watched, distinct striation is visible, something in appearance to the well-known " Newton's Rings."

If a vacuum tube is so constructed as to have another tube within it (see Fig. 18), also exhausted, with two sets of electrodes, one set for the outer tube and the other set for the inner one, no matter whether the outer tube is more exhausted than the inner one, or the inverse, provided a

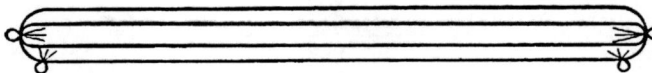

Fig. 18

spark in air of a given length would pass through either tube, it will be found, on lighting up each tube successively that bands form in each tube, which can be resolved when placed in the magnetic field (I shall refer to this subject later), and this procedure renders it more clear that there are bands in the inner tube.

If the experiment is made by joining together the pairs of electrodes at each end, then, according to the general law, particularly if the resistance of the outer tube is made less than that of the inner one, the current should travel through the outside tube, very little through the inner tube, but this is not the case.

This experiment does not contradict the general or Faraday's law, but offers what I believe to be a further proof that the glass, *i.e.* dielectric of the vacuum tube, is necessary to produce the bands; also a further proof of the present view that the current travels through the dielectric, and sinks into the conductor. The current in this experiment practically enters both tubes at the same point, and refuses to leave the dielectrics.

Now, had the inner tube been constructed of metal, would the current appear in the outer tube?

To settle this point such a tube was made, notwithstanding the structural difficulties which presented themselves. A current of very high E.M.F. (6 inch spark in air) was passed through the inner tube. Naturally the current sparked from the electrodes to the metal tube, and this latter conducted the current. At the same time the outer tube glowed, instead of remaining dark. This experiment may be described as a modified form of the " hemisphere " experiment, employed in static electricity, applied to dynamic electricity.

I think that I have so far said enough to show that the glass, for some reason or another, is an active agency in producing the bands. If I may be permitted to express an opinion which may on further experiment be modified, it appears to me that the vacuum tube has a strong analogy to the ordinary metal conductor. The glass takes the place of the dielectric, and the gas within represents the metal. The current travels along the dielectric and sinks into the gas; that is, the conductor. When the dielectric is sufficiently distant, the discharge is of a different nature and is disruptive. This latter phenomenon may be absent in solid conductors, but in any case it may not be possible to produce it, on account of structural difficulties.

Formerly, were it required to produce bands at given distances, it would have been necessary to fix, in some suitable manner, solid bodies along a tube at stated places,

bands being formed where the solid bodies were situated.
I am not aware whether any such tubes have ever been
made, for they would have been inconvenient for experiment, but in order to try the effect, I constructed two
tubes in the following manner : Each tube had a slight
glass rod placed in its axis and was supported from the
ends of the tube. In one tube little discs of glass were
placed at equal distances along the rod, and in the other
tube the discs were replaced by small glass spheres.

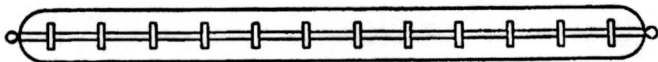

FIG. 19.

FIG. 20.

These tubes were lit up inductively, otherwise the effects
could not be produced with certainty.

These two tubes are shown in Figs. 19 and 20. It will
be observed that a bright band appears on each side of
every glass disc, but in the case of the glass spheres, it will
be found that four bands are produced on each sphere :
one on either side of the equator of the sphere, and one at
each pole.   This is worth notice, because it shows that the
sphere acts as a disc in the plane of its equator, and as a
rod the length of its polar axis.

I have no doubt that some pretty deductions could
be made from this phenomenon, which must be clearly
due to certain properties possessed by a sphere.

I might mention that, in the case of the sphere, under

no condition can bands be produced differently; provided the volume of the sphere bears a comparatively small relation to the volume of the tube. Other methods for producing bands at given distances have been employed, but they are cumbrous and unpractical.

At one time my electric energy was drawn from an alternate current source, as well as from an induction coil; but I found it possible to produce with the induction coil a current identical in nature with that produced from the alternate current source. When the induction coil is employed in the customary manner, the chief current is produced on the "break." Consequently, the tube is lit up by a current of one kind which is intermittent, the opposite current being so faint as to be barely visible, if at all, but the coil can be so arranged that the "make" current may be rendered visible. The "break" current, however, is always the most important. If the source of current supply for an induction coil has a high E.M.F., higher than that for which the coil was constructed, a resistance being inserted to prevent too much current from passing through the primary, then a different effect will be produced.

In my own case I employ a 100 volt current on a primary constructed for 10 volts. The "break spark" on the "contact maker," is then much larger, also a spark is created on the "make," and the final result is that the effects, produced in the vacuum tube, are identical with those when the alternate current was used, *i e.* the "break" current is diminished and the "make" current shows itself. This is not a condition of the coil which is unstable, but is a created condition which is a stable one and can be reproduced at pleasure in any coil.

A separate "make-and-break" apparatus is better for this class of work than the common form of vibrator. The currents used had an E.M.F. as low as 500 volts; and from this pressure to 1000 volts every phenomenon can be produced in its purity.

It must not be forgotten that, when the two currents are seen in the tube at the same time, they really follow one another. The rotating mirror will prove this to any one who does not realize the fact.

It might also be mentioned that, when very small currents are used, the discharges are in what has been termed the "sensitive state."

The exhaustion for these low pressures must not be very high, and there is no actual need that it should be ; nor is it material as to which gas is used. Ordinary air is as good as anything else. In saying this it is not meant that for certain classes of experiment high vacua and special gases, particularly the simple ones, are not desirable; but we are not dealing now with these.

Up to this point I have endeavoured only to show certain analogies between the current passing through the vacuum tube, and the current passing through an ordinary conductor such as a cable. I have not attempted to deal with the considerations which arise from the mode of propagation, or in bringing the phenomena into line with the ether theory. The latter can be done by any one having a knowledge of the subject, and I would therefore sooner confine myself to experiments and their deductions, or probable deductions.

I must remind you that the ether, or any other theory, bears a relation to Science in the same way as the fingers do to a child, when they are employed in learning to count. A theory is merely a mechanical idea to enable our imperfect minds to understand that which would otherwise be incomprehensible.

If we have at the present time, say, a million phenomena which fit in with the undulatory theory, it is quite certain that there are millions of other phenomena unknown to us, numbers of which may not agree with that theory. It is, therefore, quite conceivable that the time may arrive when some other theory will be required in the place of the one which we believe to be correct at the present time; but to take up the position that all theories are false, and to work without one at all, is not possible. You might as well suggest a problem to be solved without going through a single mathematical operation, which is quite conceivable if the mind of man were perfect; but no one would suggest the abolition of mathematics on the ground that the perfect mind would not need it. For this reason any school which rejects all theories is doing an injury to the advance of Science.

NOTE.—Since the experiments described were performed, many new kinds of interrupters have appeared, such as the "mercury jet," "electrolytic," and others. Their use simplifies in some degree the arrangements for making the induction coil produce given desired results

PART II

I now propose to turn to the second part of the subject, which to many workers may be more attractive, namely, the behaviour of electric currents in the magnetic field.

In order to carry out these experiments, Messrs. Nalder constructed a large magnet from my designs, and I have to congratulate this firm on the admirable manner in which all the details have been carried out. An illustration of this apparatus is given in Fig. 21. The weight of the magnet is about 13 cwt., and the arrangements are thoroughly practical. In every detail it is a departure from the old Faraday type.

The great magnet which Faraday employed was but a rough instrument which he would probably have modified when building another. I found it very difficult to work with this type of apparatus, and therefore decided to build one on engineering lines. In this magnet the poles can be approached and receded by screws, and small pole-pieces of various types can be fixed to the poles in the same manner as is done in the case of chucks on a watch-maker's lathe. Hollow poles also exist with microscope and polariscope fitted. The suspension device is very convenient, and removable at pleasure. Switches for making both poles alike, and for commutating the current are added, in addition to the usual switch for making and breaking the current. Before breaking the circuit a resistance is

20

placed in parallel with the coils, and this is done by the

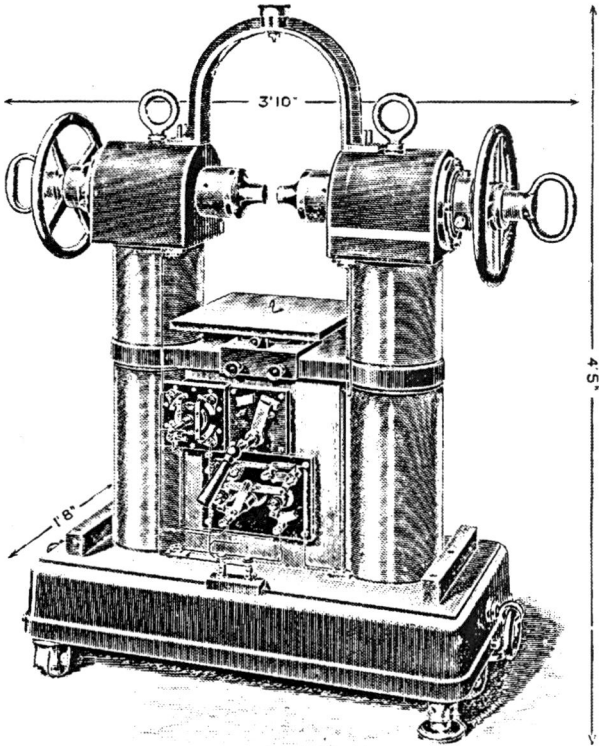

FIG. 21.

movement of the main switch, and not by a supplementary one.

The illustration (Fig. 21) shows the magnet with the

glass case removed. There are many pieces of supplementary apparatus, one of which converts the magnet into a huge D'Arsonval galvanometer. The magnet is excited with three amperes from 100 volt circuit.

To this date very little appears to have been published on the effects produced upon electric discharges in rarefied gases when placed in the magnetic field. That certain effects are produced under such conditions is known, but not much more has been published, as far as I can ascertain. The rotation of the discharge about the pole of a magnet is also known.

Experiments have likewise been made to show that there is a slight displacement of current in a conductor, when placed in the magnetic field. I believe this was shown many years after the effect had been seen in my laboratory on a much larger scale than that which was published.

I will now describe certain phenomena shown by vacuum tubes in the magnetic field.

The tubes as generally made are of little service for this purpose. Those which have already been described are better, also tubes about 300 mm. long and 16 to 25 mm. in diameter, with suitable brush electrodes, the object being to obtain distinct bands at some given convenient distance apart. The E.M.F. employed in connection with these tubes is very low, rarely exceeding 1000 volts, and the induction coil is arranged to give effects in the tubes the same as if an alternate current had been employed from a transformer.

If such a tube as described (see Fig. 22) is placed between the poles of the magnet when excited, one pole being north and the other south (Fig. 23), the two currents separate in the tube equatorially.[1] The appearance is that of an unlit tube with two lines of bands clinging to the

[1] See Appendix for meaning of "equatorially" and "axially."

tube.   (See Fig. 24, the dotted lines indicate the position
of the bands.)

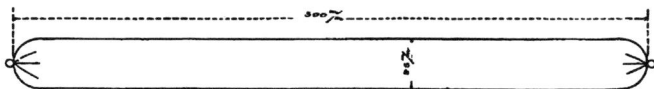

FIG. 22

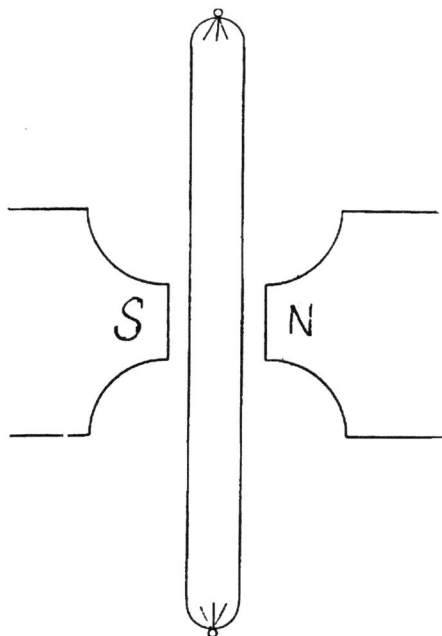

FIG. 23.

I will describe the appearance more minutely; for
convenience let it be assumed that the two currents are

visible in the tube. There will then be seen the two lines
of bands placed equatorially. On examination it will be
observed that the only difference between the column of
bands on one side and those on the other is in the direction
of the convex sides of the bands.

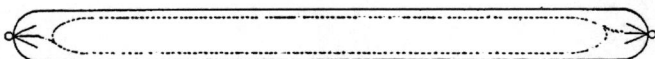

Fig. 24.

Consider only one side : it will be noticed that the
bands become smaller and smaller as they approach the
strongest portion of the field. At the same time they
approach one another until the bands appear to be a mere
line of light, yet with a magnifying glass the bands can
be still observed.

Fig. 25 gives a rough idea of what takes place. Only
one line of bands is shown.

It is therefore evident that the two currents tend to

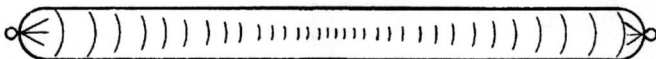

Fig. 25.

pass out of the magnetic field, and each current takes a
definite position in regard to the field. If the current in
the tube is reversed the appearance in the tube will be
the same, that is, similar currents occupy the same
positions, but if the poles of the magnet are reversed,
the convexities of the bands reverse also, *i. e.* the currents
change sides.

That the currents are separated is certain, but the
absence of light in the centre of the tube, *i. e.* in the
strongest part of the field, may be due to three causes, if

not more. It may be that the resistance of the gas has been increased, and the current therefore travels at places of less resistance, or the resistance of the gas may remain unaltered, and it is simply that the two currents desire to take up a particular position in regard to the field, or both conditions may exist.

A tube under these conditions will show a higher resistance when the magnet is excited than when unexcited, but on reflection this is not necessarily a proof that the resistance of the gas is actually increased. It may be a spurious increase in the resistance.

It must not be forgotten that a magnet is equivalent to a current travelling in a circular conductor, and that the current travelling through the tube is one in a straight and movable conductor.

In other words, this experiment is a pretty and convincing proof of Ampère's theory as shown with movable conductors, which has hitherto been made in a different and more clumsy manner.

It appears to me that the true explanation why the two currents move out of the field. is due rather to this Ampèrian explanation than to the actual increase in the resistance of the gas.

If the induction coil is now supplied with another source of current, having a lower E.M.F., the usual state of things is produced in the tube, which can be so arranged that only the break current becomes visible. On placing the tube in the field, only one column of bands will appear and not the two. Whether the arrangements are such that one or both currents are visible in the tube, on reducing the current considerably the time is reached, when although the tube may be lit throughout when held outside the magnetic field, yet on placing the tube between the poles, the passage of the current ceases.

This would indicate at first sight that the resistance of
the gas is increased. Consequently, in the first experiment described, not only did the currents tend to take up
definite position in respect to the field, but an increased
resistance of the gas assisted the phenomenon. Another
consideration may also enter, and it will be referred to
later.

I am unable to say positively whether this is the case
or not, but my various experiments lead me to think that
when the current is exceedingly small, the reason why it
does not pass through the tube when under magnetic
influence is due to the current being, so to speak, "crowded
out," *i. e.* driven as it were into the glass of the tube, which,
having such a high resistance, stops it passing, as far as can
be observed, on account of the low E.M.F. of the current.

There are a large number of other interesting experiments which can be made by holding this tube in various
positions, below, near, and around the poles of the magnet,
but as they can all be reduced to the principles I have
mentioned, I will not occupy more time in describing
them, beyond giving a few diagrams to show what occurs.

I have already described the appearance of the tube
when placed between the poles N. and S, when the
magnet is excited.

If, now, the current is turned off the magnet, the
magnetism falls gradually, and the successive stages of
the phenomena will manifest themselves in the tube from
the strongest field to zero. This is the best method of
making the observations, on account of the process being
gradual.

Figs. 26, 27, 28 and 29 show the various phenomena
when the tube is between the poles, the bands seen in
Fig. 29 are their position when the magnet has lost its
field, and Figs. 30, 31 and 32 illustrate the appearance

FIG. 26.

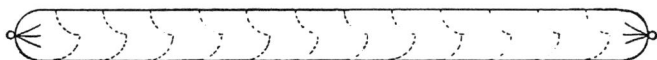

FIG. 27.

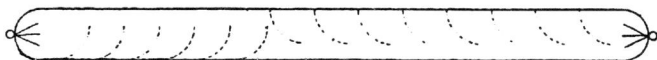

FIG. 28.

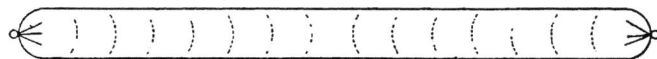

FIG. 29.

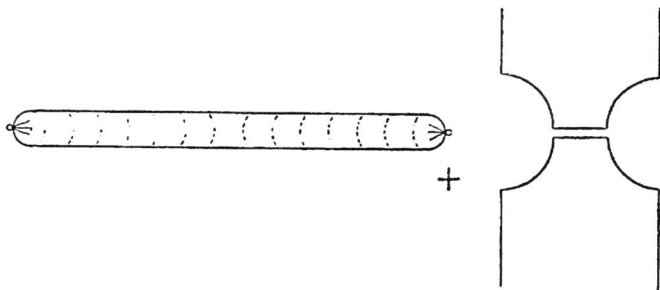

FIG. 30.

of the tube in other positions near the magnet when excited.

C

One important use is open for vacuum tubes. It is that
of exploring the magnetic field of dynamos, alternators,

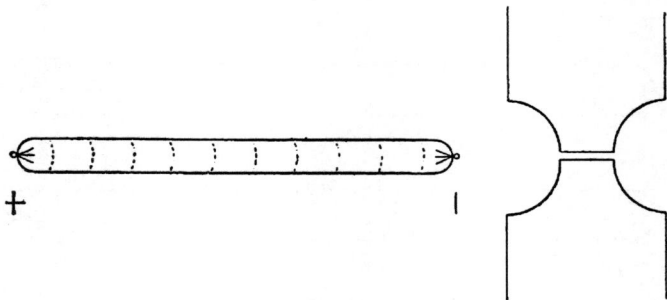

FIG 31.

or for any other class of practical work of this nature as
well as for theoretical investigation. A very small coil
and tube will suffice for such testing.

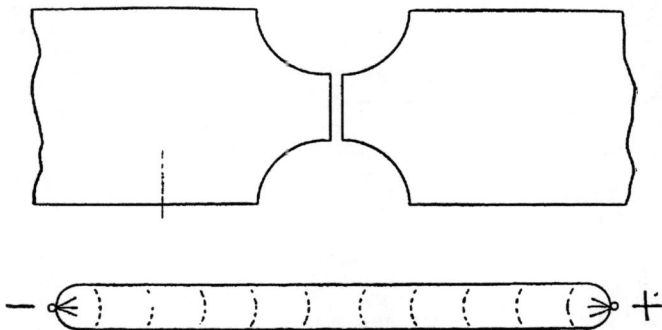

FIG. 32.

It is desirable to point out, that when there is a free N. and S. pole, anywhere in the proximity of the tube there are banded lines of light on each side of the tube when the two currents are present, and a single band of light when only one current is present, and the position taken up will always be situated equatorially to the lines of force. Consequently the position of the light in the tube is the test for lines of force.

The smallness of the bands, and their closeness, gives the strength of the field.

Considering for a moment one line of bands, in all cases this line will be straight when the field is symmetrical. When unsymmetrical the line will be bent into various curves, generally spiral.

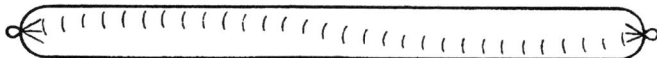

FIG. 33.

By this method of testing, the field can be mentally mapped out in a few seconds, without the necessity of employing the various apparatus as at present used, where the results have to be set down and plotted before any idea can be formed of what is going on.

Fig 33 roughly illustrates the appearance of the tube when held in an unsymmetrical field.

We will now examine what phenomena occur when the tube is placed between the poles of the magnet and the current is increased by raising the E.M.F.

If the current traversing the tube is gradually increased, although the two columns of bands will still be there, the "Waist," so to speak, becomes widened, and a faint light shows itself throughout the remainder of the tube.

Continue to increase the current. and if all the conditions

have been suitably arranged, *i. e.* the magnetic field
sufficiently powerful, the amount of current nicely adjusted,
and the tube is of suitable diameter, then there will
suddenly start out between the poles, and within the tube,
bright lines which can only be described as apparently the
lines of force becoming visible. If this experiment is
carefully made, the lines of force are very brilliant and
unmistakable. Indeed, the effect is better shown than in
the old manner with iron filings, because it is exhibited

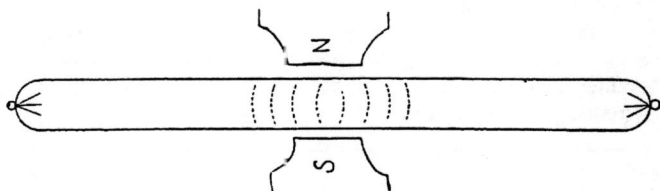

FIG. 34.

FIG. 35.

in a three dimensional manner. Fig. 34 is a general
diagram, and Fig. 35 illustrates the actual appearance of
the tube, *i. e.* the apparent lines of force are shown in the
centre of the tube, also the bands.

It is well known that the current passes with greater
freedom with the lines of force than across them.

The experiment showing the lines of force appears to me
a further proof of this phenomenon. I also regard it as a
strong evidence that my view as to the formation of the
bright bands is correct, namely, self-induction.

When the current has to cross the lines of force in the stronger portion of the field, it meets with more resistance. You have therefore a tube containing a conducting material with varying resistance. It is quite conceivable that heat may be developed in sufficient quantity, when crossing the stronger portion of the field, to render any finely-divided matter present sufficiently heated to become visible, and that the reason why the imaginary lines of force appear actually as lines, may be due to self-inductive effects, similar in character to those which formed the bands under normal conditions, that the lines are really bands taking upon themselves the form of the lines of force. It would then appear that it is possible, even probable, that the apparent increase in the resistance of the gas in the tube is due to two causes; firstly, the current or currents, if two are present, tending to take up a position outside the field; and, secondly, that the current or currents prefer to evade crossing lines of force, in order to find a path of less resistance. Consequently it does not follow that the actual resistance of the gas has become increased. It is still a spurious effect. Analyzing the conditions more closely, if the current is driven out of the field equatorially, then the increased resistance which would be offered to the current when crossing the lines of force is greatly diminished, because the current in this case is in a weaker field. This is true probably for small currents, but for larger ones the field must be made much stronger than can be done in practice to produce the effect.

For a long time past it has been known that bismuth shows a higher resistance, when placed in a strong magnetic field ; I believe that Faraday was the first to show this phenomenon for the metal named, and Professor Sylvanus Thomson to publish the fact for other metals.

It will be evident, after describing the vacuum tube

experiments, that another explanation is possible for this
apparent increase in the resistance of metals when placed
in the magnetic field. It is clear that the methods which
can be employed to prove either of these cases run entirely
in parallel, and that the question would still remain an
open one as to which is the true explanation, were it not
that in the vacuum tube, the experimenter can actually
see what is going on in a rarefied gas, and to some extent
the same phenomenon occurs in metals, as shown by the
experiments I have made, and I am strongly of opinion
that the resistance of the metals is not really increased,
but it is simply the current or currents which are pushed
out of the field, and tend to take up a position of equili-
brium, combined with the traverse of the lines of force,
which gives the apparent result of increased resistance,
which, in fact, may be due to the current traversing a
smaller section of the area.

If this be true, a curious circumstance must be noticed.
Generally speaking—I do not know whether it is true in
all cases—the bad conducting metals appear to increase
their resistance more in the magnetic field than is the
case with those which are better conducting. I have found
this result with many metals. It might therefore be
assumed that the current when crossing the magnetic
lines of force in bad conducting metals, can move with
greater freedom than is the case in better conducting
metals.

I think it more than probable, that if a careful series of
experiments were made, on various metals placed in the
magnetic field, it would be found that there is no simple
relation between the resistance of the metal and the
strength of the magnetic field, except for a given current.
This, indeed, would be one of the best proofs to uphold
the view which I believe to be correct, but I have so far

not had the opportunity of pursuing this part of the subject further.

To turn to one or two practical deductions, which may almost be termed commercial, depending on this phenomenon, but having no bearing as to which theory is correct, I may give two examples which will suggest many others.

Take the case of a coil in an alternator or a direct current machine, which is continually passing through powerful magnetic fields. It must be clear that at one moment the current is being driven, as it were, out of the copper, and the next moment, when passing through a weaker field, the current density at every portion of the section of the copper is more or less the same. In other words, there is what may be termed a pulsating of the current in the copper from without to within and the inverse, during the time that the coil or the magnets are in motion, as the case may be.

. It would therefore appear, that apart from any other conditions which may exist, there must be some slight pulsation or period in the direct current as well as in the alternative current, due to the cause mentioned.

The copper in all armatures, therefore, should be larger in section than needed by theory to meet this variation, which, however, is exceedingly small, and the margin of safety at present allowed more than suffices for the purpose.

To give another example, it seems obvious that it is undesirable in the D'Arsonval galvanometer to make the field too strong. A point must be reached when the amount of current is so greatly reduced in the swinging coil, that the instrument becomes less sensitive. This is admirably shown on the large magnet, when arranged as a D'Arsonval galvanometer. The magnet is excited, and the position of the dot of light observed when a very small

current is passed. On breaking the circuit of the magnet,
the magnetism falls, and the dot of light indicates a much
larger deflection, the E.M.F. being kept constant on the
galvanometer coil terminals. This experiment can be
made in another way by leaving the magnet excited
and placing a resistance so as to reduce the current
flowing in the field circuit, when a similar result is
obtained. There are other reasons why the field should
not be made too strong, yet my experiments lead me
to the conclusion that those referred to are the main
causes for loss of sensibility under such conditions.

If the magnet is so arranged that both poles are made
N. or S., and then a thick plate of iron is laid across them,
and upon this plate a pole is stood upright, you obtain the
equivalent of a bar magnet; one pole pointing upwards,
the other pole being the base of the instrument. It will
be found that if the vacuum tube, with which most of the
previous experiments were made, is placed over this pole,
the effects are the same as when placed between the poles
N. and S., but the phenomena are not quite so pronounced.
This result could easily have been anticipated, because the
lines of force close to the pole travel much in the same
way as when the poles were opposite one another with the
tube between. It is, however, instructive ·to trace the
lines of force with a vacuum tube, when the magnet is
arranged as mentioned.

The phenomenon is considerably altered, if the magnet
is now arranged so that the poles are N.N. or S.S., and the
tube is placed between them. Currents within the tube
take up their positions separately as in the case when the
poles were N. and S., but now the lines of bands will be
placed axially, and not equatorially, as before. Moreover,
the lines of bands cross one another in the strongest portion
of the field. This is shown in Fig. 36, where to avoid con-

fusion, the lines of bands are simply represented as dotted lines. If the tube is placed below the poles the bands will appear as in Fig. 37 ; if above, as in Fig. 38, the difference

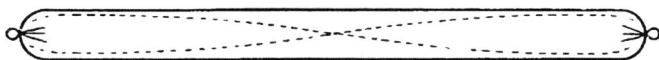

FIG. 36.

being that they face the reverse way. If only one current is employed in the tube, then the appearance of the bands, when placed between N.N. or S.S., is very similar to that of an unsymmetrical field, which it really is. This is an

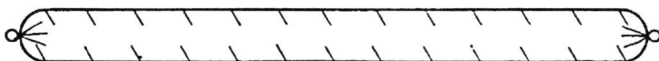

FIG 37.

instructive experiment in many ways, and particularly if the tube is used to trace the field.

A very pretty experiment is that of taking a vacuum tube about 16 mm. diameter and 500 mm. long, and bending it almost into a circle, then holding it over the

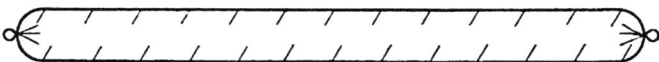

FIG. 38.

poles of the magnet when N. and S. The appearance of the bands will then be as shown in Fig. 39. Observe that the currents cross at the strongest portion of the field. Although the N. and S. poles are employed in this experiment, the phenomenon in the circular tube is very similar to that in the straight tube, when placed between N. and N.

It may also be noted that if the tube containing a metal tube, which was mentioned earlier, has one electrode placed in the magnetic field, the spark from *each* electrode to the metal tube is divided into two, equatorially, as if the currents traversed the metal tube separated, which appears thus to be proved.

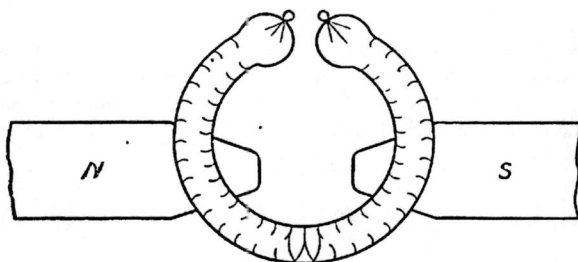

Fig. 39.

From many of the foregoing experiments, it appeared to me possible to take an alternate current and separate it by magnetic means into its two constituents, *i.e.* two pulsating direct currents. That such a current can be split up by other methods is well known, but they are not simple, nor can any very instructive deductions be made from them. The separation by the magnetic method is very interesting, for quite apart from the analysis of the alternate current, a neat illustration is given of many well-known laws.

We have seen how the two currents become separated in the magnetic field. It appeared to me therefore probable that if a glass septum were placed in the tube with which the experiments referred to were made, such a division not reaching to the electrodes, the currents would be completely separated in their course. The equivalent to this construction would be a double tube. I therefore constructed tubes of the shapes given in Figs. 40, 41, 42.

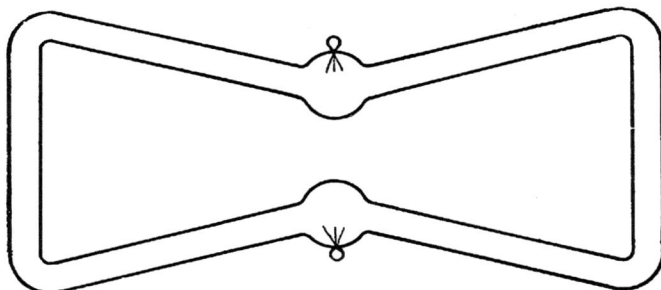

Fig. 40.

Then, in the case of any of these tubes, if one of the bulbs containing an electrode is placed in a strong magnetic field, the plane of the tube being placed equatorially, complete separation is evident from the fact

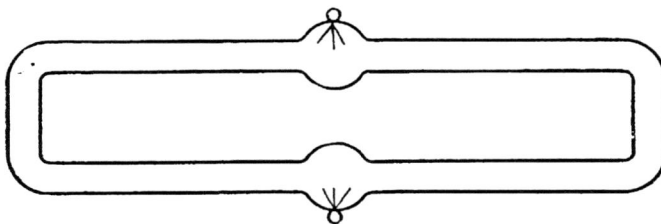

Fig. 41.

that there is but one line of bands in any portion of the tube.

It is interesting to note that if one of these tubes, say Fig. 41, which is about 150 mm. in length, is placed equatorially, and the current so adjusted that when the field is excited no current passes, on the tube being turned out of the equatorial plane, the current makes its appearance. With the tubes mentioned, if the excitation of the field is permitted gradually to drop, the various stages of the phenomena are very distinct, *i. e.* from the

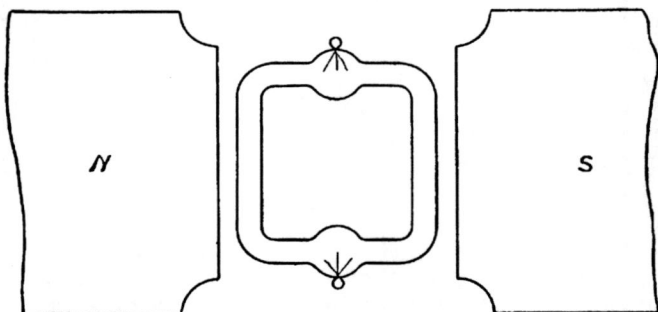

Fig. 42.

alternate current traversing throughout the tubes to the moment when the current becomes separated into two pulsating direct ones. There is also a stage when the

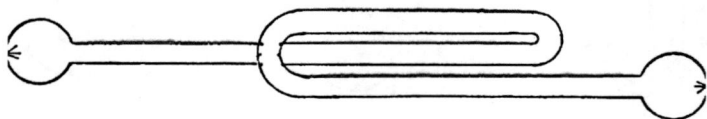

Fig. 43.

discharge appears to be spiral, but I think this is probably an optical illusion.

In the bent tube, as shown in Fig. 43, if the curled portion is placed in the magnetic field, the spiral discharge is very well shown.

The experiment was varied by employing two tubes as shown in Figs. 44, 45. The end electrodes were joined

FIG. 44.

together in each case. The middle electrode in Fig. 44 is centrally situated; in Fig. 45 it is nearer to one end. If no separation of the current took place, it is clear that in tube Fig. 45 most of the current would take the shortest course, but when the electrode in the body of the tube in each case is placed in a strong magnetic field, the current

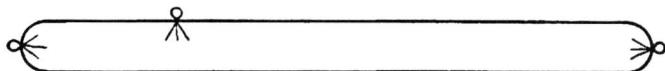

FIG. 45.

travels to the two ends in single lines of bands. The discharge is very pretty, for the reason that there is a glow of light very much like a fountain, in addition to the lines of bands.

Carrying this method of experimenting a stage further, I employed a tube U-shaped, as shown in Fig. 46. The two electrodes at the free ends of the tube are joined together, and a third bulb containing the other electrode is placed in a strong magnetic field. If the current is suitably adjusted, only one line of bands (each due to a current in one direction) appears in each arm of the tube.

Going a step further, another similar tube is taken, and

the free ends joined by two wires, as shown in Fig. 47. On passing the current it becomes visible in ·the second tube, and this current can be analyzed in another strong magnetic field. In each case only a single line of bands will appear in each arm. It is quite immaterial how long

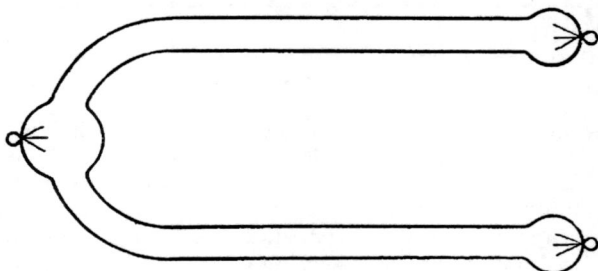

Fig. 46.

the wires joining the tubes may be. This experiment is not easy to perform on account of the care required in adjusting the current, but when this condition has been complied with, the phenomenon is unmistakable.

This experiment may be a forerunner of a new system of electric lighting by the employment of alternators with

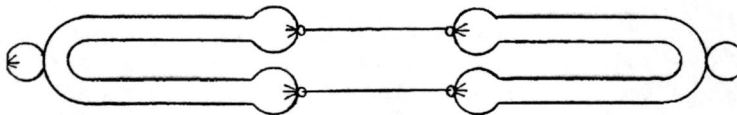

Fig. 47.

a service system of a direct pulsating current, without the employment of moving machinery for re-dressing. At present I am only able to deal with very small currents.

In order to be sure of the ground, these experiments were conducted not only with an induction coil arranged to show the two currents in a tube, but also with an alternate current from an alternator, with similar results in each case.

As it is now generally recognized that a current advances through a liquid and through a gas in a similar manner, I therefore thought it desirable to repeat the experiments which were conducted with tubes of the shape of Fig. 46 with a water tube, and examine the result. Fig. 48 illustrates the tube used, the portion at

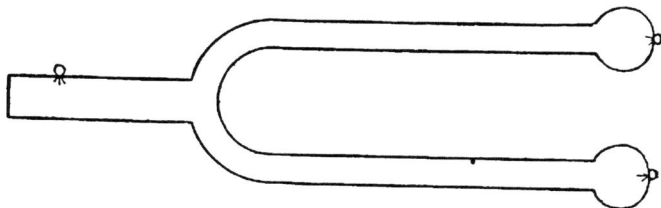

FIG. 48.

the bend of the U being open. This end of the tube was placed between the magnet poles, and the tube was joined up by means of wires to an analyzing tube, as shown in Fig. 47, which was placed between the poles of another powerful magnet. The difference observable in the nature of the discharge between the excited and unexcited condition of the magnet which influenced the water tube, was barely noticeable. There was a slight change in the appearance of the discharge in the analyzing tube, but no more can be said. This experiment has no direct bearing upon the manner in which the current is propagated, but I regard it conclusive as showing there is not that same freedom for a current to take up a new position when traversing a liquid, as is the case with a gas, that is, fluid is not a true movable conductor.

If a current is made to traverse an exhausted globe of glass, say 50 mm. in diameter, with an electrode at each pole, such as shown in Fig. 49, the discharge has a similar

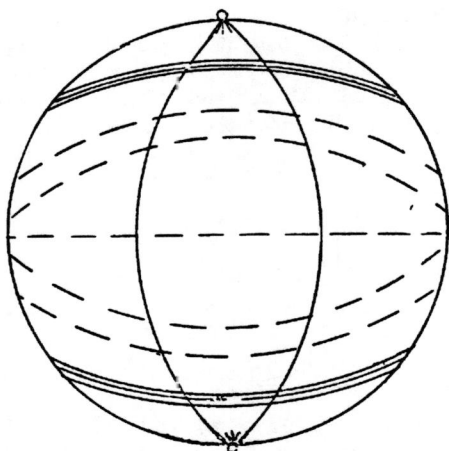

Fig. 49.

appearance to that in the electric egg. When this globe is placed in the magnetic field it presents a beautiful appearance. A purple disc is seen near each electrode at right angles to the polar axis, the planes coinciding with the lines of force at these places. The current travels between the two electrodes as two separated lines of light joined at the electrodes and considerably parted midway between them.

The current can be so adjusted that these two lines of light are so much separated that they travel nearly round the inside of the glass of the sphere. The position of the lines of force also becomes visible at all parts within this tube. In fact, this spherical tube is, in a way, a summation of the various phenomena shown in a number of the other tubes.

We are all familiar with the fact that the electric spark in air is distinctly zig-zag in form. This is not clearly visible, until the spark is made a sufficient length, and is so well shown by an induction coil.

Most workers have also tried that well-known experiment of discharging the spark from the induction coil through a very fine wetted filament, or a very fine festoon of wire, when it is observed how the filament or wire crumples into the zig-zag form, during the time the discharge is passing. It would therefore appear as if the zig-zag form of discharge is not dependent on the fact that the current passes through the air, but rather that there is a tendency for the discharge to be zig-zag when disruptive, and can be shown when the conductor is free to move.

If the experiment of showing the magnetic lines of force in a vacuum tube is performed with the E M.F slightly raised, there will appear throughout the tube a number of line discharges zig-zag in form very similar in appearance to the ordinary spark in air.

In this instance there can be little doubt that the magnetic field, as well as self-induction, plays a part in the phenomenon. I would venture to suggest that in all cases the zig-zag advance of the current may be due to its own magnetic influence, combined with self-induction, since it is unlikely that the magnetism of the earth is sufficiently great to produce any visible result in this direction.

To examine this phenomenon further :—

The air in a vacuum tube is only rarefied in comparison with air at normal atmospheric pressure; thus, air in the latter condition may also be regarded as rarefied when compared with air under greater pressures.

Consequently it is not improbable that striation may be produced in gases at all pressures, provided a sufficiently high E.M.F. is employed, and the conditions made favourable for the formation of bands. The zig-zag discharge

Fig. 50.

may therefore be the tendency for the current to form striation, and a compromise is brought about, resulting in the uneven line of light; the self-induction of the current assisted by its own magnetic field being the primary cause.

If an electric spark between two points of, say, 10 or 12 mm. apart (see Fig. 50) is placed between the poles N.

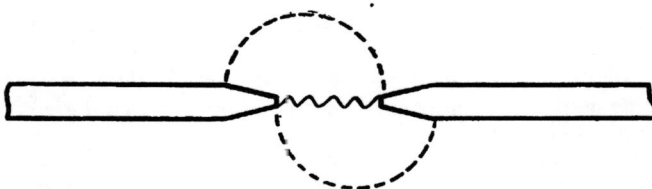

Fig. 51.

and S. in a powerful field, one of the poles being hollow so that the effect can be easily observed, then the following phenomena result: If the coil is arranged to give the two currents in almost equal proportions, the appearance will be that of Fig. 51. The spark will appear bluish-white, and two reddish sparks will appear, one on either side, giving the appearance of a letter D, on one side, and a reversed D on the other ; the semi-circular portions do not

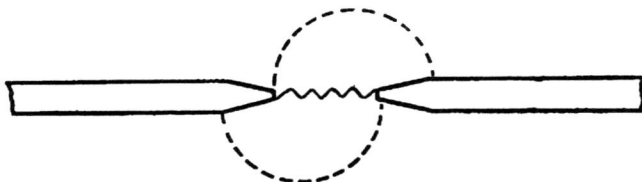

FIG. 52.

form a circle, being somewhat displaced.   If the current is reversed, the same phenomenon is produced, but the displacement is inverted.   See Fig 52.

FIG. 53.

If the coil is arranged to give practically only the break current, the appearance will be as in Fig. 53, and when reversed as in Fig. 54.

FIG. 54.

It is evident that since the supplementary arcs follow the variations mentioned, they must be electric discharges or currents and not chance flames.

In connection with this subject, there are a large number of other very interesting experiments, but they will be dealt with at some future time.

I started with the belief that vacuum tubes would prove a useful aid for investigating electric phenomena, and I also felt assured that for many purposes they could be turned to practical account. I already employ them to a considerable extent for the rapid examination of magnetic fields for adjusting galvanometers in which the magnetic field forms a portion of the apparatus, and for a variety of other purposes.

I hope that those who have had but little faith in vacuum tubes on account of their distant acquaintance-ship with them, may be tempted to modify their views, after what I have written, and give them a trial.

I have still in hand several series of experiments which, I think, will probably be found of interest when completed, if the word completed can be applied to any subject   I simply mean a set of experiments which prove some definite point, but nothing more.

It would be interesting to examine the results described, and many others, with a steady current such as would be produced from a large accumulator.   The late Mr Warren De La Rue carried out some useful work in this direction, but though the E.M.F. which he employed was high, the currents were very small   I am at the present time constructing an accumulator of 1000 cells, capable of giving two amperes, without injury to the cells.   This E.M.F. is more than is required for almost every experiment described. I therefore hope to obtain some new and interesting results.

I have tried here to express myself freely without any regard to the orthodox opinions which prevail at present.   It is most likely, therefore, that I have "run off the rails" at many points.   It is sometimes convenient to do this, in order to make explanations clearer, and avoid in this manner long descriptions, studded with still longer parentheses. The advantage also exists that it helps the worker to look at things from different points of view, which may be described as the Romance of Science.

APPENDIX

FOR the convenience of experimenters who are interested in the subject of phenomena in vacuum tubes, I add this Appendix, to give some information on the apparatus I employ.

The high speed contact apparatus consists of a star wheel with twenty spokes, the end of each spoke being tipped with a platinum stud.

A platinum-tipped spring is touched as these spokes pass, and the star wheel can be rotated by means of an electro-motor at the rate of 2500 times per minute or more without failure of contact. I do not in practice employ more than 1500 breaks per minute.

The apparatus for slow makes and breaks consists of a rod with platinum-tipped ends, working in guides, this rod having a sliding action given to it by means of a revolving eccentric which is moved by an electro-motor.

Two posts, platinum tipped, are placed on the stand which carries the apparatus, one at each end, and the ends of the rod strike these posts alternately, and thus the makes and breaks are produced.

To make sure of contact, and to avoid vibration, the platinum blocks at the ends of the rod are mounted on coach-springs, which in their turn are supported by spiral springs. The speed of the makes and breaks with this apparatus is at the rate of 800 per minute, which can be lowered to 400 at pleasure.

Condensers are used in connection with both these instruments, so that they are very free from sparking.

The current passes through both these instruments and thence to the primary of a suitable, and carefully made, Apps Induction coil. A switch permits either the rapid or slow "contact breaker" to come into play at pleasure. The current used for the primary circuit is 100 volt direct current.

A variable resistance is placed in connection with the coil primary for adjusting the current.

A variable resistance is also placed in the secondary circuit.

The length of spark which I employ in most of the experiments is only 0·17 mm. The E.M.F. measured upon a Kelvin electro-static-volt-meter is approximately 700 volts with the rapid breaker, but by altering the pressure of the spring on this contact breaker, thereby making the break more or less sudden, this voltage could be brought down to 600 or raised to 800 at pleasure.

If the speed is increased, the E.M.F. rises in the secondary circuit to the limit of 1200 volts in these experiments. With the slow breaker the E.M.F. varied from 300 to 400 volts.

In describing the behaviour of vacuum tubes in the magnetic field, the words "equatorially" and "axially" occur. To prevent misunderstanding, by "equatorially" is meant a direction at right angles with the axis of the poles; and "axially," in the direction of the axis of the poles. If the lines of force be considered as an imaginary approximate sphere, then the meanings of the words become obvious.

CPSIA information can be obtained at www.ICGtesting.com
Printed in the USA
LVOW06s1921020314

375754LV00019B/895/P